Beautiful Cities

Coloring Book

RAND McNALLY

Beautiful Cities

Designer: Michelle LeBlanc-Smith
Copywriters: Erika Nygaard, Joella Morris
Design Production: Erika Nygaard
Product Management Director: Jenny Thornton
Production: Carey Seren
Artwork by Shutterstock Images.

Designed by Rand McNally
Skokie, Illinois 60077

Printed in U.S.A.
March 2016
PO# 45147
ISBN 0-528-01580-X

If you have any questions, concerns or even a compliment, please visit us at randmcnally.com/contact or e-mail us at: consumeraffairs@randmcnally.com or write to:

Rand McNally
Consumer Affairs
P.O. Box 7600
Chicago, Illinois 60680-9915

randmcnally.com

Introduction

Relax and color a cultural journey!

Are you ready for the trip of a lifetime? Discover 62 beautiful cities—from Buenos Aires to Paris to Marrakech—in this collection of stunning and intricate color-ready illustrations. Whimsical city maps, lively street scenes, local architecture, and intricate, culture-inspired patterns await your creative touch to bring them to life.

Rand McNally's travel experts selected the world's most beautiful cities for your coloring journey. *Beautiful Cities* will inspire you with more than 60 scenes to color, including 15 extra wide illustrations. Each illustration features unique world cultures, architecture, art, and iconography for you to explore.

Not just for kids anymore, sophisticated coloring books have been discovered by teens and adults of all ages as an effective way to reduce stress, calm the mind, and escape from the digital world. Let your imagination soar as you explore the world of coloring. You will amaze yourself with your creations!

Bon voyage!

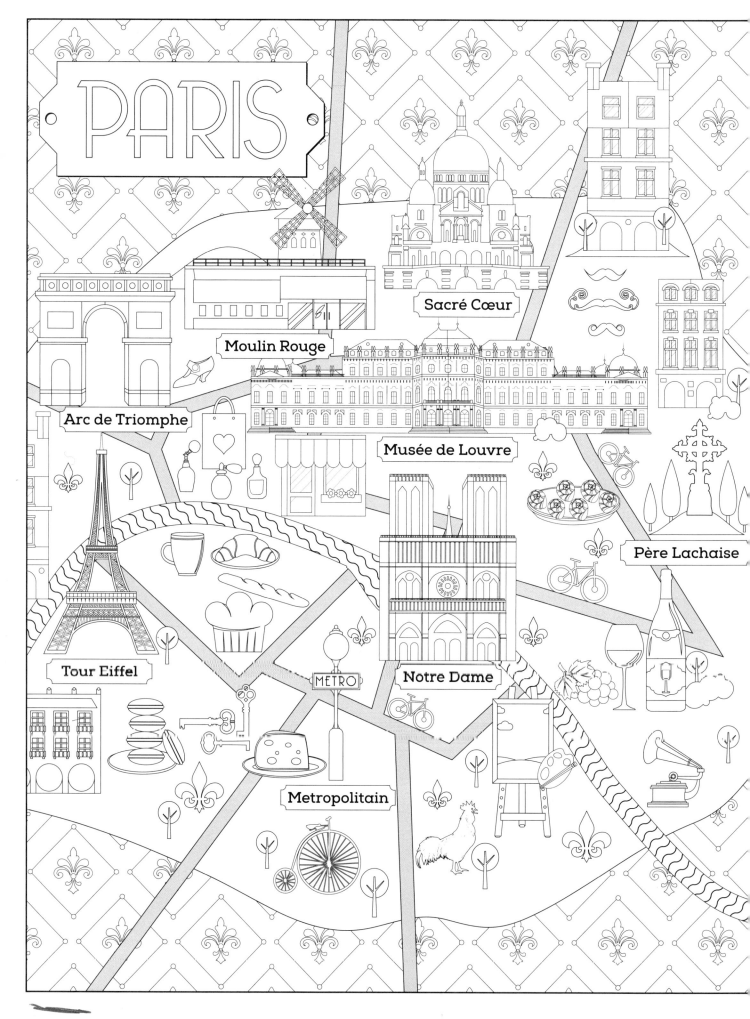

PARIS

Sacré Cœur

Moulin Rouge

Arc de Triomphe

Musée de Louvre

Père Lachaise

Tour Eiffel

METRO

Notre Dame

Metropolitain

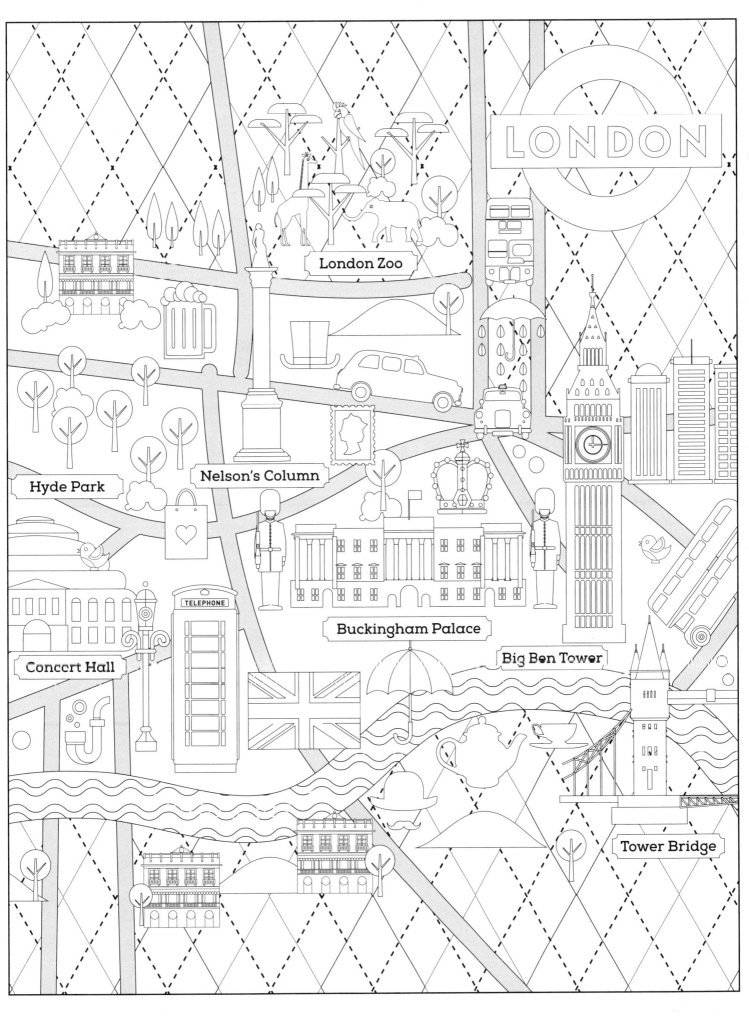

LONDON

London Zoo

Hyde Park

Nelson's Column

Concert Hall

TELEPHONE

Buckingham Palace

Big Ben Tower

Tower Bridge

LOS ANGELES

AUSTRALIA

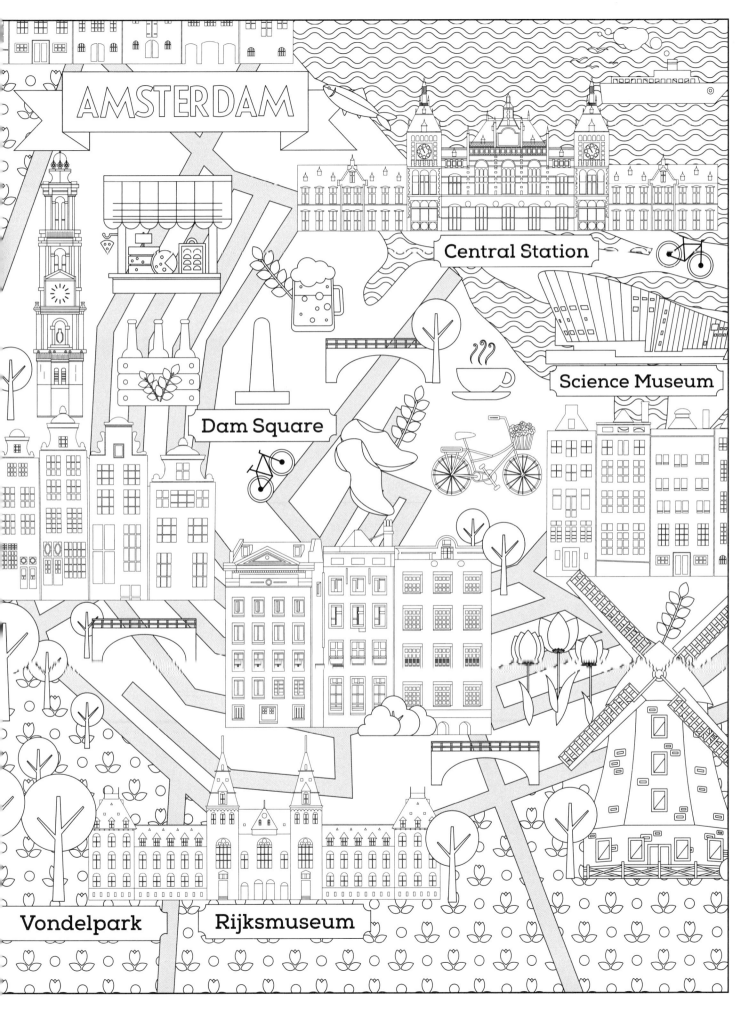

AMSTERDAM

Central Station

Science Museum

Dam Square

Vondelpark

Rijksmuseum

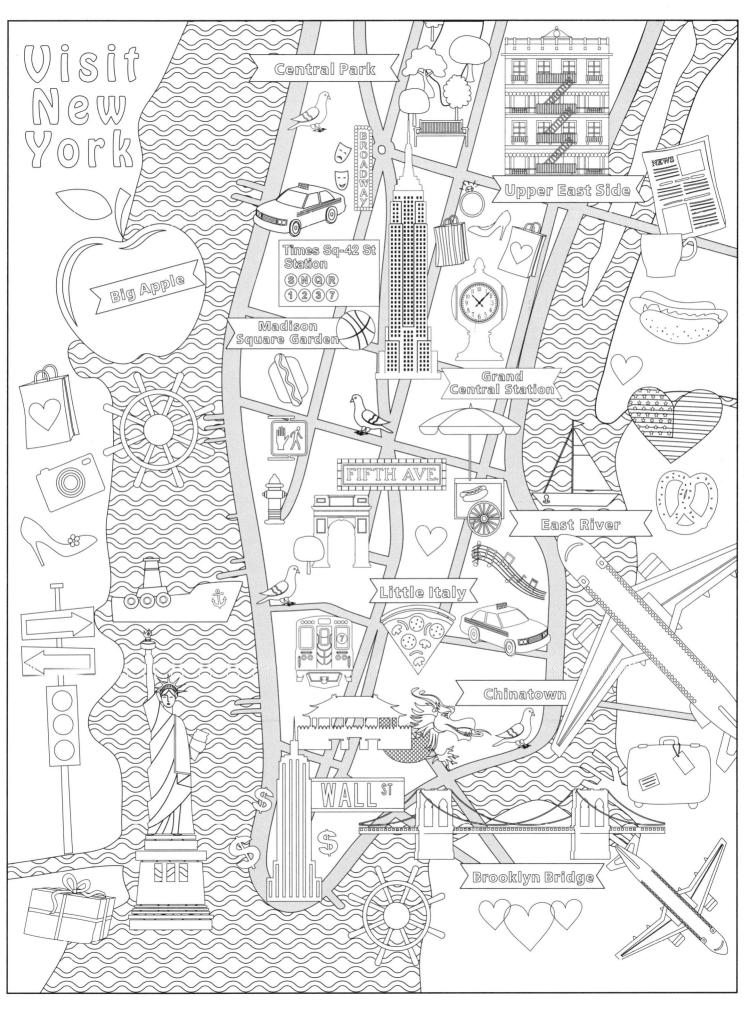

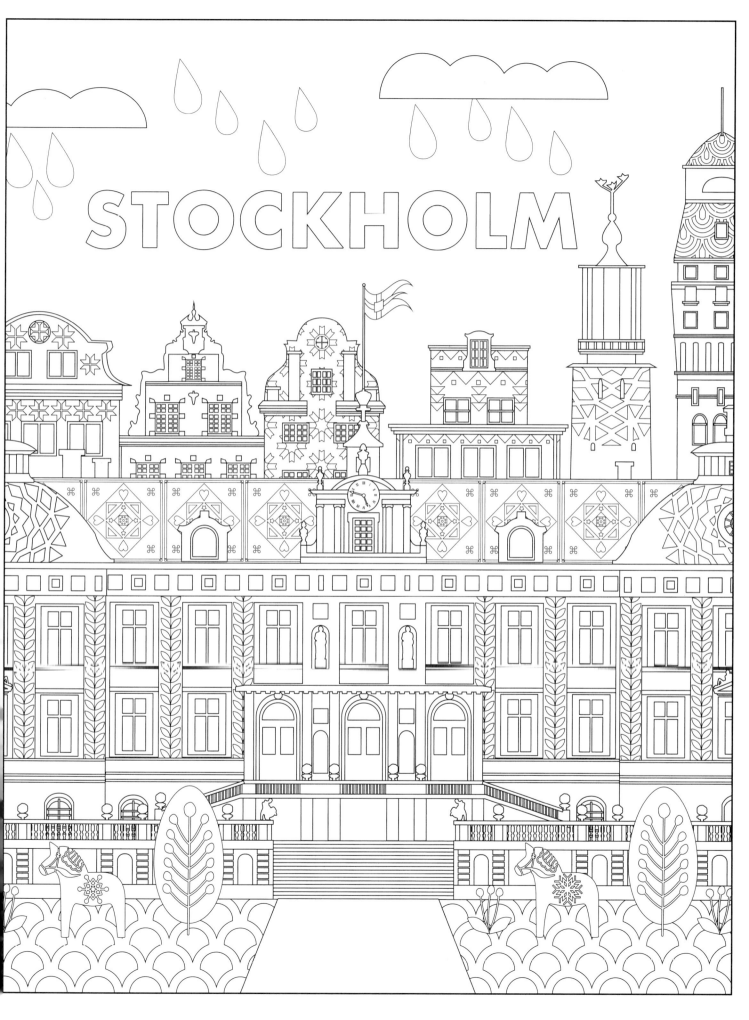

RUSSIA

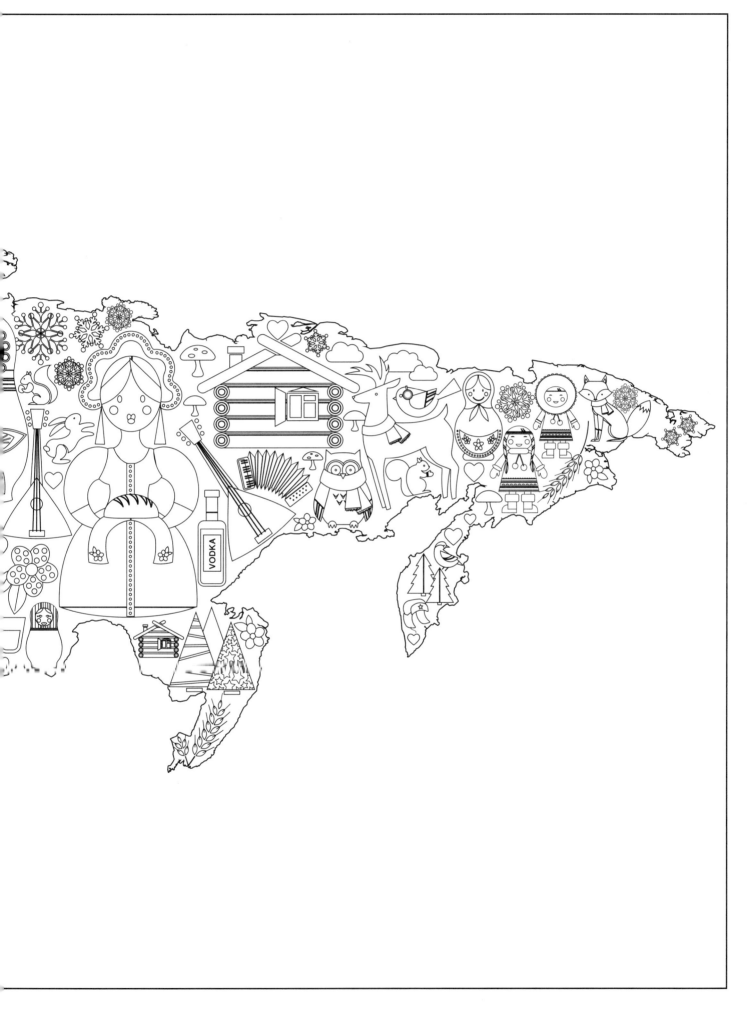

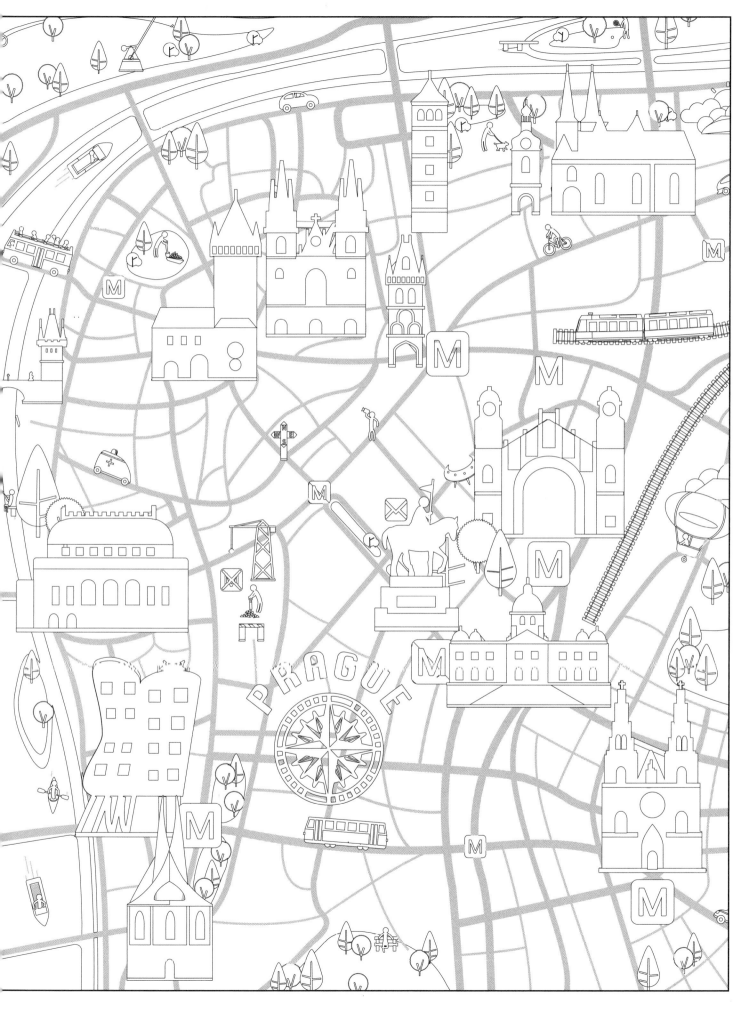

TURKEY

Cairo
& Giza

KUALA LUMPUR

Thailand

Buenos Aires